Mind over Matter

Introduction

Truth of the Matter

When it comes to describing MATTERS, it varies. According to the webster dictionary," Matter is defined as a subject of interest or concern. Events or circumstances of a particular situation; the substance of which a physical object is composed; an indefinite amount or quantity; to be of importance. There are more definitions listed however these definitions I have listed applies to this self-help guide.

Truth of the matter is we often allow such person, place, or thing to give us meaning or existence in which we suppose to give matter meaning of existence in which we suppose to give matter meaning of existence. Why is it opposite? Well, that is because we got our priorities backwards and our culture renders great value upon us if we possess some things and live above the average means. We are validated by our accesses and our achievements and places in which we resign or dwell. This clearly conclude that we are weighed by these "Matters". We wake up motivated by the assumption that if we accomplish any one of these people, places or things, we are becoming closer to self-fulfillment or

whole.

As a matter of fact, by the "American Dream "suggests that material lavishness, or reality is shaped and molded from those concepts. What usually transpires is our psychological being becomes overwhelmed with these perceptions and eventually turns into a part of our reality.

Truth of the matter, it's not our reality at all, it is our "American Cult" of reality that is sprung on us.

 Now I am not against the American dream of what we believe is success is, but I am against the material world effecting our judgement, our sanity, and state of mind. This self-help book is written to encourage and strengthen **"mind"** control over **"matters"**. **If we were able to think with a clear conscious, we would have less complications in our lives. Allow this book to provide some methods to apply so life can become less stressful.**

Strain our thinking of the mind with drug addiction. When a physician prescribes drugs for sickness and/or illness, that's because diagnostics tests has been performed. As we know, sickness and illness are defined as something detrimental to our health that can result in death. Drug and alcohol do not only alter our way of thinking, but it also becomes a physical need as well, like what was discussed. The physical aspect for drugs and alcoholic hunger is more intense by the mind (limbic system) creating urges that become a need for drugs and alcoholic substance consumption. But in all actuality the mind seeking for that fulfillment that correlates with our body eventually created some sort of need for drug and alcohol. Once the mind and body become alter with a superficial feeling then is stored in our mind (limbic system) as a pleasurable feeling and then urge for that feeling again.

That then is how we become addictive to a certain feeling not to an actual drugs and alcohol. To go back to the physical need for drugs and alcohol, by the consumption of substance, our body began having tolerance for drugs and alcohol. Before I begin explaining about the physical effect of our body, I must inform you about the mind and body connection.

Our mind is what sends messages to our body to perform yet the body at times resists the idealist mind because of its need for constant hydration and nourishment. The mind conducts through the body until the mind snoozes for so many hours to recuperate while our body follows suit. After the daily abuse of substances consuming alcohol for so long, the brain began to deteriorate and in some cases the body suffers as well. This is referred to as a functional/dysfunctional addict. What happens to the brain eventually registers the substance or alcohol as a dependable substance and when it is absent of such substances, it causes the brain to malfunction and subsequently the body malfunction as well. Yes, it is a consequential thing when the mind does not have no control over the types of matter (drugs and alcohol).

Let me speak on another matter like (sex, gambling, material things, food addictions, and feelings) These types of matter that influence in a different way versus an actual substance. that recommend therapeutic measures including group interaction. However, this self-help guidebook would be a covenant of what's already provided for these matters. This self-help guidebook provides convenient effective recovery. I would like to say that "the matter" I am referring to are emotionally driven because it all effect or emotional well-being.

The brain is placed into two different categories. One side of our brain controls our logical/reasoning side, and the other side of our mind/brain controls our emotional side. I do not want to confuse none of you readers, but I am urged to put in a simple perspective so you can identify with both sides of our mind/brain and how it works.

Everything we learn is self-taught or by someone else or something. Such information is stored and eventually applied and used in our lives. But on another note, that's why it is important on who we follow and learn from. It can be difficult to relearn something after you've been taught incorrectly. Our feelings are among a broader range of things because we are naturally emotional creatures. We are created out of intimacy which is derived from emotion and passion that engulfs our DNA make up. So, you see our first nature is love, which revolves around emotions. Educating ourselves falls under our logical and reasoning side of our mind/brain/cortex. We often struggle to understand our emotional side because emotions are a powerful force in our lives. Unlike logical thinking, we aren't taught how to manage feelings; instead, we experience them naturally from birth.

 We are created out of feelings/emotions in which I explained how it is our first nature. Our nature shapes how we express ourselves and impacts on our well-being.

For these reasons alone, it influences our lives, whether we intend it or not. It Is fair to say that we lack control over our emotional side of our mind (brain) because of the natural irrational complexities that fall under emotions and feelings. This title "Mind over Matter" are by far the most difficult task to master. By this world being driven by material objectives, our personal interest rises for that occasion which enhances our emotional yearning for material things. Mind you, matter can be blindly identified externally and internally. Love, lust, cravings, etc. are shaped around these emotional sentiments in which we tend to become emotionally attached. Our brain is divided into two hemispheres, one logical and one emotional. In the world that we live in, we also develop a desire for material means that eventually develop in us a sense of values by having material possessions.

We also discover by having and/or obtaining material things that it is also used to gain favor with individuals. Nevertheless, materialistic things give people prestigiousness, which then make you what "they say, a model citizen in today's society".

Now the reason I explained the whole materialistic perspective is because in our days of living it is a way of winning. America has set the bar so high by our culture amplifying material things as success. The greater our financial income, the more material things we buy to become relevant and important. So, what happens is that the brain/mind inherits this concept that feeds into our subconscious as well as consciousness drives off that idea. Achieving better education in or to get higher paying jobs. Our minds absorb everything around us, especially during childhood. Once we become of age to acknowledge the power of material things (matter) it is when we then shape and mode our perception on the value of material things. The impact that matter has on the human mind made our reality consistent to what emotionally drives most. Being emotionally attached to material things or the thought of a thing greatly influences us. Now you should understand why mind over matters are so hard to master.

Our minds identify material things as pleasurable consumption through our limbic system. By our pleasure consist of the emotions nature, it outweighs our reasoning (cortex). This self-help guidebook will provide you with methods and tools that will be effective in mastering mind over matters. **Instinct thinking versus critical thinking.** Instinct thinking can be described as somewhat impulsive acts that don't use thought into something. It's normal for us to think less about daily routines like using the bathroom, doing daily house chores, and bathing ourselves, other than that, our day is moving according to daily agendas set outside our homes. I want our readers to do me a favor. Consider what you were doing before opening this self-help guide. As a matter of fact, it would probably be more meaningful if you think about what you have accomplished today that was productive or meaningful. Ok now that you have, how productive or may I say, how many things have you got done that were on your 'to do list'? I know you may not have wrote out a short term "to do list" nor a long term one, but I'm quite sure you got it stored in your head what you must do withing a week that you stagnated to get done because of other preoccupation "matters".

I would like to use reading a book scenario. The average person who reads a 200-page book only reads a minimum of 30-40 pages daily. Yet and still, it will take a few days to finish unless it's a timeframe required on reading the book.

It takes longer than 1 to 2 days because our attention span is limited and our brains aren't used to sustaining intellectual activity. When they say, "if you don't use it, you will lose it", that is so true in all retrospect. That goes for our physical as well as our mental. Now, I will go back to the book example. Our instincts play a dominant role in how we participate in things.

The easier the task, the less require for us to think matters out. This causes us to use less of the productive side of our brain. Instinct thinking also requires less cognition. We often engage in trivial pursuits rather than activities that demand intellectual effort. This subject is included under the main title of this book, indicating that the issues discussed are either difficult to resolve or challenging to fully understand. By a book stimulating us we still choose not to use our brain to fullest capacity. So, you see we put off reading a productive book just to avoid exercising the brain. We get mentally exhausted when using concentration skills if we use less instincts, we will have less problems in our lives. Why? Because our brain will use more of our intellectual side of the brain that consists of higher intelligence. Our brains are so used to leaning more on our emotional sentiment side for pleasure, it entertains desirable matters as something that is more important. Moving away from pleasurable, emotion-driven thoughts isn't always negative, but it becomes a concern when it prevents us from leading a healthier life or making wise decisions.

 Priorities due to the struggling mind with these issues, it has a hard time with understanding our priorities, of what comes first, what is more important. One brain as we understand in having two sides are definitely very complex. One side governs logic and reasoning, while the other manages emotion and affection. Like what was explained earlier in this self-help guidebook, the emotional side will always play over our critical thinking because we are created out of emotions even if it is only a very small percentage, it is inevitable. By, it at times confuses our brain with the mind being overlap with these inevitable emotional complexes. We are left to believe in one thing or another by receiving great benefits and/or great pleasure means. For example, by us having sex that produce a "feeling of pleasure", it offset our reasoning emotional impulses. When we are confronted with a choice, we often gravitate toward physical pleasure. Because the emotional sensational side of our brain that result in us obtaining means to become values as well as attractive to win over the man or woman we are interested in.

 This is why it is often stated that individuals may lose motivation to pursue their goals once they have established relationships with the person of interest.   But I got the right tools to keep our objectives intact without compromising our integrity or morals. Stay abroad and keep reading. Bad experiences (confusion of changed mind over matter) – This is pertaining to different things and so the answers vary. Overall, it is always something or someone that overrides our clear perception and rationale. People, places, or things that are considered important often end up being blamed in certain situations. Sometimes, certain experiences can trigger negative feelings that distort our views of people, places, or things.

Yes, bad experiences tend to impact our lives to where it alters our perspective on people, places, or things. Although personal experiences often cause us to overlay emotions onto our rational thoughts, we often believe we're relying solely on reason or a mind-over-matter approach. In fact, "matter is still" in control of our thinking and ultimately our actions.

People, place, or thing are usually responsible for emotional vulnerability when we become emotional attach to a person, place, or thing. That is what causes us to guard ourselves so we can prevent undetermined outcomes from experiences. However, our feelings will inevitably rise occasionally. But still, we think we're in control or manage situation in a reasonable manner. Because we have had our share of experiences of people, places, and things; we tend to assume we're in control now. Little that we know being affected by something isn't always obvious nor visual. How we respond or react to certain things can be sometimes all mental. I will explain how to exert mind over matter to overpower the very thing(s) that manipulate us. Dealing with someone or something a certain way can be develop through certain experiences we may had with such "matter". Bad experiences can have our mind operate with precaution, so we won't get emotionally involved. However, it appears that we use rationale. It's just by making approaches we tend to believe that method will give us a better result in a situation. Having an interest in something draws emotional attention. Emotions are our core being. The matter of something gets less credit on why we are motivated for various reasons. Temptation according is the act of enticing to do wrong by promise of pleasure or gain, provoking risks of something or someone, to induce to do something. This all should seem familiar because we all have been under the dumb of each other and/or something that describe one of the above scenarios. This definition describes matter over mind in a perfect sense. For example, I remember when a friend of mine got access to the answer sheet when we were in sixth grade and I was struggling on taking the test for that subject. He then offered me the answer sheet, and I accepted with no hesitation. I was emotionally attached to the fact that I will pass a test, and I would not have to worry about if it's a chance I don't pass. So, you see the answer sheet (the matter) totally took over my reasoning concerns of consequences. I was emotionally invested in passing a test that caused me distress. This example equates pleasure into passing that was encouraging to cheat in something that will eventually reflect my perseverance.

Most incidents involving drugs and alcohol addiction requires some sort of recovery convention program that recommend therapeutic measures including group interaction. However, this self-help guidebook would be a covenant of what's already provided for these matters.

 This self- help guidebook provides convenient effective recovery. I would like to say that "the matter" I am referring to are emotionally driven because it all effect or emotional well-being. The brain is placed into two different categories. One side of our brain controls our logical/reasoning side, and the other side of our mind/brain controls our emotional side. I do not want to confuse none of you readers, but I am urged to put in a simple perspective so you can identify with both sides of our mind/brain and how it works. Everything we learn is self-taught or by someone else or something. Such information is stored and eventually applied and used in our lives. But on another note, that's why it is important on who we follow and learn from.

It can be difficult to relearn something after you've been taught incorrectly.   Our feelings are among a broader range of things because we are naturally emotional creatures. We are created out of intimacy which is derived from emotion and passion that engulfs our DNA make up. So, you see our first nature is love, which revolves around emotions. Educating ourselves falls under our logical and reasoning side of our mind/brain/cortex.

 We often struggle to understand our emotional side because emotions are a powerful force in our lives. Unlike logical thinking, we aren't taught how to manage feelings; instead, we experience them naturally from birth. We are created out of feelings/emotions in which I explained how it is our first nature. Our nature shapes how we express ourselves and impacts our well-being.

For these reasons alone, it influences our lives, whether we intend it or not. It Is fair to say that we lack control over our emotional side of our mind (brain) because of the natural irrational complexities that fall under emotions and feelings.

This title "Mind over Matter" are by far the most difficult task to master. By this world being driven by material objectives, our personal interest rises for that occasion which enhances our emotional yearning for material things. Mind you, matter can be blindly identified externally and internally. Love, lust, cravings, etc. are shaped around these emotional sentiments in which we tend to become emotionally attached.

 Our brain is divided into two hemispheres, one logical and one emotional. In the world that we live in, we also develop a desire for material means that eventually develop in us a sense of values by having material possessions. We also discover by having and/or obtaining material things that it is also used to gain favor with individuals. Nevertheless, materialistic things give people prestigiousness, which then make you what "they say, a model citizen in today's society". Now the reason I explained the whole materialistic perspective is because in our days of living it is a way of winning.

 America has set the bar so high by our culture amplifying material things as success. The greater our financial income, the more material things we buy to become relevant and important. So, what happens is that the brain/mind inherits this concept that feeds into our subconscious as well as consciousness drives off that idea. Achieving better education in or to get higher

This self-help guidebook will provide you with methods and tools that will be effective in mastering mind over matters.

Instinct thinking versus critical thinking. Instinct thinking can be described as somewhat impulsive acts that don't use thought into something. It's normal for us to think less about daily routines like using the bathroom, doing daily house chores, and bathing ourselves, other than that, our day is moving according to daily agendas set outside our homes. I want our readers to do me a favor. Consider what you were doing before opening this self-help guide.

 As a matter of fact, it would probably be more meaningful if you think about what you have accomplished today that was productive or meaningful.

Ok now that you have, how productive or may I say, how many things have you got done that were on your 'to do list'?

I know you may not have wrote out a short term "to do list" nor a long term one, but I'm quite sure you got it stored in your head what you must do within a week that you stagnated to get done because of other preoccupation "matters". I would like to use reading a book scenario.   The average person who reads a 200-page book only reads a minimum of 30-40 pages daily. Yet and still, it will take a few days to finish unless it's a timeframe required on reading the book. It takes longer than 1 to 2 days because our attention span is limited and our brains aren't used to sustaining intellectual activity. When they say, "if you don't use it, you will lose it", that is so true in all retrospect.

That goes for our physical as well as our mental. Now, I will go back to the book example. Our instincts play a dominant role in how we participate in things. The easier the task, the less require for us to think matters out.

This causes us to use less of the productive side of our brain. Instinct thinking also requires less cognition. We often engage in trivial pursuits rather than activities that demand intellectual effort. This subject is included under the main title of this book, indicating that the issues discussed are either difficult to resolve or challenging to fully understand.

By a book stimulating us we still choose not to use our brain to fullest capacity. So, you see we put off reading a productive book just to avoid exercising the brain. We get mentally exhausted when using concentration skills if we use less instincts, we will have less problems in our lives. Why?

Because our brain will use more of our intellectual side of the brain that consists of higher intelligence. Our brains are so used to leaning more on our emotional sentiment side for pleasure, it entertains desirable matters as something that is more important.

Moving away from pleasurable, emotion-driven thoughts isn't always negative, but it becomes a concern when it prevents us from leading a healthier life or making wise decisions.

Priorities due to the struggling mind with these issues, it has a hard time with understanding our priorities, of what comes first, what is more important. One brain as we understand in having two sides are definitely very complex. One side governs logic and reasoning, while the other manages emotion and affection. Like what was explained earlier in this self-help guidebook, the emotional side will always play over our critical thinking because we are created out of emotions even if it is only a very small percentage, it is inevitable.

Though at times, our brain becomes confused with the mind being overlap with these inevitable emotional complexes. We are left to believe in one thing or another by receiving great benefits and/or great pleasure means. For example, by us having sex that produce a "feeling of pleasure", it offset our reasoning emotional impulses.

When we are confronted with a choice, we often gravitate toward physical pleasure. Because the emotional sensational side of our brain that result in us obtaining means to become values as well as attractive to win over the man or woman we are interested in. This is why it is often stated that individuals may lose motivation to pursue their goals once they have established relationships with the person of interest.   But I got the right tools to keep our objectives intact without compromising our integrity or morals.

Stay abroad and keep reading. Bad experiences (confusion of changed mind over matter) – This is pertaining to different things and so the answers vary. Overall, it is always something or someone that overrides our clear perception and rationale.

People, places, or things that are considered important often end up being blamed in certain situations. Sometimes, certain experiences can trigger negative feelings that distort our views of people, places, or things. Yes, bad experiences tend to impact our lives to where it alters our perspective on people, places, or things. Although personal experiences often cause us to overlay emotions onto our rational thoughts, we often believe we're relying solely on reason or a mind-over-matter approach.

 In fact, "matter is still" in control of our thinking and ultimately our actions. People, place, or thing are usually responsible for emotional vulnerability when we become emotional attach to a person, place, or thing. However, our feelings will inevitably rise occasionally. But still, we think we're in control or manage situation in a reasonable manner. Because we have had our share of experiences of people, places, and things; we tend to assume we're in control now. Little that we know being affected by something isn't always obvious nor visual. How we respond or react to certain things can be sometimes all mental. I will explain how to exert mind over matter to overpower the very thing(s) that manipulate us. Dealing with someone or something a certain way can be develop through certain experiences we may had with such "matter".

Bad experiences can have our mind operate with precaution, so we won't get emotionally involved. However, our feelings will inevitably rise occasionally. But still, we think we're in control or manage situation in a reasonable manner. Because we have had our share of experiences of people, places, and things; we tend to assume we're in control now.

Little that we know being affected by something isn't always obvious nor visual. How we respond or react to certain things can be sometimes all mental. I will explain how to exert mind over matter to overpower the very thing(s) that manipulate us. Dealing with someone or something a certain way can be develop through certain experiences we may had with such "matter". Bad experiences can have our mind operate with precaution, so we won't get emotionally involved. However, it appears that we use rationale. It's just by making approaches we tend to believe that method will give us a better result in a situation. Having an interest in something draws emotional attention. Emotions are our core being.

The matter of something gets less credit on why we are motivated for various reasons. Temptation according is the act of enticing to do wrong by promise of pleasure or gain, provoking risks of something or someone, to induce to do something. This all should seem familiar because we all have been under the thumb of each other and/or something that describes one of the above scenarios. This definition describes matter over mind in a perfect sense.

For example, I remember when a friend of mine got access to the answer sheet when we were in sixth grade and I was struggling on taking the test for that subject. He then offered me the answer sheet, and I accepted with no hesitation. By doing so I pursue taking the test with using the answer sheet to pass or get a passing grade. Now with the initial thought, I wrestled with or may I paying jobs. Our minds absorb everything around us, especially during childhood. Once we become of age to acknowledge the power of material things (matter) it is when we then shape and mode our perception on the value of material things. The impact that matter has on the human mind made our reality consistent to what emotionally drives most.

 Being emotionally attached to material things or the thought of a thing greatly influences us. Now you should understand why mind over matters are so hard to master. Our minds identify material things as pleasurable consumption through our limbic system.

 By our pleasure consist of the emotions nature, it outweighs our reasoning (cortex) say contemplated on accepting the answer sheet from my friend. I remember thinking to myself, I will guarantee pass and I would not have to worry about it if it's a chance I don't pass. So, you see the "matter" (answer sheet) totally took over my reasoning concerns of consequences.

I was emotionally attached to the fact that I will pass a test, and I would not have to worry about if it's a chance I don't pass. So, you see the answer sheet (the matter) totally took over my reasoning concerns of consequences. I was emotionally invested in passing a test that caused me distress. This example equates pleasure into passing that was encouraging to cheat in something that will eventually reflect my perseverance. The example was not about me obtaining answer sheet, it was me picking matter over rational thinking. We often believe at times that obtaining pleasure at all costs gratifies us but develops into a vice.

Just from my early ages of receiving that answering sheet, it was concluded through my childhood experience I then start developing "matter over mind" syndrome. As easy for us to have the reason to cheat, is as easy for us to apply that same mentality in other "matters" in our lives. Once we believe we'll receive pleasurable benefits, it is when we base our interest around something or someone. Getting accustomed to doing things the easy way usually relieves our thinking endeavors.

 Thinking endeavors can be the cause of stress which lean towards the easy way of doing things. Also, we really have a problem with choosing the mind over matter because of the above scenarios or similar reason(s). People, place, and things can have emotional bondages on us that stem from many reasons relating to our inner being.

But we cannot be a slave for our lower body parts desires that beneath our head that's symbolic to our rational cognition side. The goal is to empower our mind to make rational decisions. Provoking by the rational of our thinking, we continue to see the resistance that occurs by the other side of our brain capacity that consists of emotion, lust and desirable ties. By gaining deeper insight into how our brain and mind operate, we can better grasp the fundamental concepts related to both hemispheres of brain function. Our lower self originates from and is controlled by the limbic system, which is found on one side of the brain.

When such "matters" become valuable over time due to pleasing experience we develop emotional interest in person, places and things. By the world we live in shape and mode our perception on things is why and how we draw interest into establishing value for things. Our culture defines standards and values for almost everything. Growing up in this culture places a strong emphasis on achieving material success. Eventually we develop this self-gratification concept that undermines precautionary behavior and reasoning. By these thoughts are encouraged by our limbic system, it stimulates our brain to form emotional connection for such things and people that enhance us in one way or another.

Seeing, consuming things that we develop interest in, I give us a feeling of pleasurable sensation. When we find ourselves in situations where we need to distance ourselves from certain people or things, it often troubles us deeply, even if doing so isn't in our best interest. Resisting is difficult when we're emotionally attached, and I see it can affect us negatively.

Detaching ourselves from something or someone and I realize it can have a negative impact on us. Detaching ourselves from something or someone we became emotionally attached to is a hard task. However, stay tune to methods of exercise.

<u>Mind of Matter</u>

Distractions can be managed through effective practices that help us control our impulses. One of the strongest forces in the world is love. I do not think it is nothing that can exceed the power possessed in a person than love. I have extensively explained numerous parts of this book what matter consist of and the role it plays in our lives.

Matter comes in all shapes, sizes, and forms in which people, places, and things are defiance of matter. The forms of matter provide objectives that give meaning and purpose to the mind. It can be internal, mental, external, or physical.

Matter can fill our minds and dull our reasoning.

Our minds are induced by all sorts of matters. It not only fulfills an important role within us, but its absence leaves us feeling incomplete.   When we seek pleasure from material possessions, life may seem empty without those things or the people associated with them.

 Once again, our culture tends to value material things. Our culture also makes obtaining things (matter) rewarding and disturbing when we can't obtain it. With our nature of love being used to put forth effort in obtaining such matters, we entertain uncertain thoughts by love being irrational and unpredictable.

 For example, once we are under control of our desires like drugs, which is form of matter, we do the unthinkable to obtain it I want to give you some scenarios on how our culture give abundance of value to all sorts of 'matter".

When we first meet someone, it is often their physical appearance that draws our attention. Then eventually we make conversation pertaining to our likes and dislikes, common interests, hobbies, career, occupation. What we usually put emphasis on is our great achievements, accomplishments and what we have materially, that is what captures our attention because this is a material world. To live a luxury lifestyle is usually the goal for Americans in general.

Another example is when we apply for loans, vouchers, credit, or any source of funds advancements. A standard bank assesses it based on set loan criteria and regulations. This process is what renders us back confirmation of proof through checking out what we claim on our loan applications. To improve our chances of securing a loan, we will be asked to provide details about all assets, gross income, and annual profit, which helps determine our net worth.

This evaluation can define our value based on material access, shaped by people's thoughts and feelings. This situation illustrates why we are uncertain about our core values. This concludes that we can become hypnotize for the glamour of things (matter) which is a prime example of matter over mind. These scenarios all validate my point about matter being over mind consumption to meet model citizen expectations.

Priorities are something that we describe as putting one thing before another. In the world we live in today, priorities will be difficult because of what already causes confusion with our values, morals, ethics because of the material (matter) needs and wants.

Due to the misconceptions about material things, a simple sheet of paper that states our credentials of achievement can be more important than our family and friends. A relationship with a wealthy associate can be more important than our relationship with our family and friends. Lots of people would pick their boss events over their cousin's birthday events.

 The point I am trying to make is what is more a priority and/or important, basing it on grounds of what was explained about the material gain which would be from the first examples. Credentials can be more valuable because what it may weigh on our financial gain versus family being more valuable and having no materialistic gain.

Second example, going to my boss event with the motive that it would be beneficial to a promotion. So, you see picking that event over your family event does not have any material impact.

From us who cannot differentiate one from another's values, it will be hard to distinguish the mind from the matter. Our constitutions have also diluted or created confusion today, especially in America with this material value system. Sorry to say, the title of a person outweighs the equivalence of all human beings.

By this system has already been in play before we were born, we still can conquer or master the power of matter. We all have experience purchasing a miscellaneous thing over purchasing something that is needed or mandatory. What happens is due to all the misperceived of our culture values it sends a message to our limbic system that control our pleasures and because of these factors it often tends to mislead what is the main priority.

The mind is a terrible thing to waste especially if we do not know how to have complete mind control over matters. Matter has numerous definitions, but I like to define it as something that is the subject of concerns, feelings or action, trouble or difficulties. Better decisions could have prevented many problems in life.

Not saying our lives would be perfect, however, it would be a better outcome and less problems. It's already challenging when the mind struggles to maintain emotional connections with various people, places, and things. Rational decision making is derived from our cortex, and our emotional side is deriving from our limbic system which drives and urges reward for pleasure. Symbolically our mind is responsible for our logic/reasoning side, and our pleasure/emotional side is responsible for our needs and wants that's developed over time through experiences.

Collective experiences are subsequently stored in our brain/mind that feed our limbic system receptor with pleasurable urges. Pleasures may include food, sex, drugs, alcohol, and other substances that satisfy physical desires, as well as material goals shaped by cultural expectations.

"Matter" is defined in different shapes and forms. Once our body and mind develop a dependable need/want is when a great percentage of our lively hood become codependent for people, places, these things.

What distinguishes the reasoning versus pleasure side is that the pleasurable side is not just personal develop interest for something. The limbic enhances emotional attachment for things that's done through experiences that really define personal interest in something and/or someone. In addition, when you are accustomed to receiving pleasurable fulfillment suddenly become deprived from getting it, it creates emotional chemical imbalance in the brain that disrupts the body function as well.

 Even while exerting our logical side of our mind, we still produce a small percentage of emotional involvement. When we struggle to solve something logically and feel frustrated, that frustration becomes an emotional matter. To explain further we would not be human if we could turn our emotions off at any given time. Humans were created through emotion, as both sex and conceiving a child are deeply emotional experiences. These examples demonstrate that it is impossible for humans to have complete control over their emotions.

 Feelings of pain, happiness, sadness, joy, just to name a few. Derive from emotions gestures, so keep this all-in mind so we can put it all proper perspective.

Knowing is half the battle, and this self-help guidebook will provide you with tools for when our emotions tend to cloud your decision, judgement, and logistics. Honestly can you imagine being able to answer, judge, view things with sheer logic?

That is like perceiving things with no color. However, the small percentage of the brain/mind we use according to is only 7%.

The pleasure in which we refer to (matter) does not have to start from external affairs. The primary purpose of this self-help guidebook is to empower ourselves to prevent (matter) from overtaking our rational decisions. If you don't understand the severity of mind over matter concept, you can seek reference on the end of this book with the diagram layout to depiction.

Again, matter have a variety of definitions but the ones I am referring to is the "matters" that causes the split decisions, the matter that pull us away from sheer reasoning, the matter that override or dominate logistics accuracy of answers. We often let our personal experiences influence our decisions, believing that past situations should guide our choices. In all actuality we still going off our feelings which mean the outcome can still be biased. Understand? Unconsciously the power of love, lust, and craving tend to cloud our judgement. And once we have these what they call "vices", it is exceedingly difficult to make rational decisions.

Do you know that your voices weigh in on just about every aspect in our lives? For example, once we want to change your diet because of health concerns, we still justify cheating on our diet. The temptation for something makes "matters" worse by seemingly preoccupying our thoughts. Another "matter" that is over the mind is when we find someone very attractive and irresistible and we disregard the proven facts that the person is not in our best interest. I've learned we often hold personal beliefs we think benefit us, even when evidence suggests otherwise.

There is a great deal of matter that has a tremendous amount of influence over us in general. We often become slaved by some "matters" by revolving our entire lives around it to maintain the certain feeling that it gives us. Matter can be described as sort of a material object, but it can also be as simply as an intense thought that's hard to overcome. If that's true, we face various kinds of challenges.

Drugs and alcohol use or other substances eventually become receptive to the limbic system and if it became a long-term use, the sense pleasure is developed. As a result, our thinking begins to focus on whatever brings us pleasure. Having these mysterious matters will make it difficult to live a productive and happy life. If you don't recognize some matters as a vice, you won't recognize the influence that matters have on your life. Drug addiction is a major issue with significant effects on the mind.

"Matter of Lust"

As previously discussed, matters can be described as any object, person, place, or thing. In this case, lust can be a part of our nature. I would not consider it to have a defect of any sort, but I would say it list in line with other matters that weigh down our rational decisions, judgement, and most importantly our priorities.

I don't want to undermine our natural inclination of procreation due to having lustful urges; however, it is taking a toll on us in such a destructive way. For example, by lust is tied in with sexual encounters, it is indeed tied in with today struggle of fidelity in marriages, honoring vows that is set forth in God's name. Lust cannot only destroy your relationships with others but also your relationship with God, which ultimately affect us having a healthy and moral life.

This "matter" (lust) us sheerly based off the exterior of the person who you are in a relationship with. What usually happens is there will be times in that relationship when tests occur in that relationship when certain aspects that are required to sustain a proportionate balance in a relationship and once it is not fulfilled, that is when collisions usually happen and what you felt was a great relationship falls apart eventually. The "matter" of lust is ordained to change which means your outlook of that person will too.

We cannot allow lust to play a role in our entire decision making for picking a significant other or deciding other important things.

"Matters of Fatality"

"Matter" causing fatality, person place, and things that can resort into deprivation of matter and we have some sense of dependability for it can develop fatality destructive issues. Absence of matter can complicate matters even more and perhaps get to the point where we resort into indulging in drugs, alcohol, domestic violence of and other uncontrollable issues, that would indeed require some sort of therapeutic help. Suicide and homicide can also be some potential. Let me explain what usually happens to resort to this destructive behavior.

Like what was explained, the content of matter contains power over us because we tend to become emotional attached for unnatural matter can over confuse us to the point where unnatural matters like person, place, thing become mistaken for a natural feeling and we become emotional disturbed when we are deprived of such matter and feel the need to resort in to self-medicated them feelings.

"Power of Matter"

Living in the world, we can pull in and push out substances of power whether in a productive or destructive way, it is usually determined from our knowledge of self. Matter is described in this instinct as something of substance, something of existence.

Knowing is half the battle especially when you are understanding "MATTER".

Matter can be described in two categories, and that is natural and unnatural "Matter Entities"

The natural matter is something described within us that stimulates desire, urges, needs, and wants for something or someone that makes us powerless. These emotional gestures arise when we have previously had an unusual experience with someone or something and were pleasuring or satisfying sensations that fulfill our inner void. For example, from when we were young and took our first bite from an apple and discovered the delightful taste in the fruit, it is when we developed a desire in the fruit. This will formulate a "want' for that fruit gain and that is what we call "desire".

What also happens is we build up a powerful craving for it which becomes a desirable pressure in the cortex of the brain until it is relieved of that desirable craving.

The power of unnatural "Matter" is described as a matter of something, someone outside of us that creates an urgency, a desire, a want and or need for something or someone.

The difference between the power of natural matter and unnatural matter is natural matter is an inability to be enslaved to a powerful feeling that interrupts your rational thoughts.

The power of unnatural matter is being enslaved to something or someone outside yourself that interrupts your rational thoughts.

"Matter of Drugs and Alcohol"

Drugs and alcohol have been discussed in some of the chapters in this self-help book but not in depth enough. In fact, this matter is so sentimental. This "matter" overrides all the other matter discussed in this book. This is an issue that is very intensified issue that developed into a psychological and physical issue. It varies on how drugs and alcohol are being introduced in people lives. One way it is introduced to one's lives is through lifestyle recreation and party tools.

 Another way drugs and alcohol are introduced to people lives are having secondhand information about it and or indirect experiences. What gradually happens, any intense emotion yearns for drugs and alcohol use leaving to believe drugs and alcohol compliments emotional gesture or moods. From a psychological standpoint, the mind conceives drugs and alcohol to be a dependability to function once the use become repeatedly during times of emotional outbreaks.

After so long of the constant use of the physical bearing of drugs and alcohol the user eventually develops a functional dependency for drugs and alcohol.

The **matter** of emotions is one thing, but the **matter** of drugs and alcohol is another. Once the emotional aspect discovers a chemical self enhancement, life really gets complicated. That is why drugs and alcohol anonymous program's philosophy is led to believe that we become painful powerless over self. Drugs and alcohol are the ultimate matter to overcome, in this case, you cannot measure nothing in this magnitude in mental disruption and challenges. However, this self-help book provides us with all the efficient tools.

"Matter of Anger"

What we know anger is to be a disrupted emotion that could cloud our judgment and also what this self-help guide for the overall teaches us that all suggested matter that clouds our judgment so by this matter being a extinct of its own natural entity of clouding more of our judgment, make matter more difficult to masters control.

For instance, my girlfriend and I attended a party together. At one point, she left to join her friends, and after she did so, a man approached her. Seeing my girlfriend and the guy in a deep conversation instantly made me furious.

I departed from the party immediately, without consideration for how my girlfriend would return home or any concern regarding her safety.

As you see, just from this natural expression of emotion came a line of spiraling bad episodes that eventually lead to the breakup of my relationship. If I had simply taken a moment to analyze the situation with rational skills, I would likely still be in my relationship. Rational thinking comes from one side of our brain that desensitizes our feelings in emotional situations.

When we are consuming with a natural expression as anger it is not easy to control especially if you exercise the expression of emotion all your life, it will take more than great methods to master control over such a natural emotion gesture.

"Detachment of Matter"

From reading this book it explains how "Matters" became so relevant to our lives and how it is so effective to how we think, how we feel and ultimately what we believe is essential to our well-being.

Your psychological development is not always easy to reframe from such mind set, it will take your desire for change, discipline, dedication and determination to change from our former mindset to the new frontier, of a new mind, of new world, and new life.

"Self-value and self-esteem over Matters"

One of our greatest challenges is being comfortable with self and that can derive from childhood.

We have our most challenges when we are a child by the simple fact we struggle with identity crisis and categories. Being the one who picks on another or being the one who gets picked on. Being the subordinate or insubordinate.

There are so many complexities and uncertainties while growing up that it makes decisions harder about what we want to be when we grow up and what is cool or not cool. Peers that eventually compliment us steer our ideology on life objectives. Once we acknowledge the advantages of having material possession (matter), that is when our self-values and self-esteem is really challenged. Material things (matters) empower us if we don't have self-worth, self-esteem and or self-values. Allow me to present methods to help us distinguish one from another and makes "matters" powerless.

"Instinct matter over mind"

Matter is not only tools of dictatorship, but also of impulses behavior that have us think-less towards just about any and everything. What usually happens is we develop a sense of intuition because of the confidence that material brings. Instincts are described as behavior below the level of consciousness. Impulsive behavior and irrational thinking upon situations. Matters make things more difficult to use cognition because matter occupies our minds. Instincts do not make matter better by far, as a "matter" of fact, matters falsify self-esteem, self-courage, and other pretenses that enable us to believe in something without knowing we are believing in the effect that matter have in our lives.

First Exercise

To begin such exercise, it starts within us by acknowledging that we have issues in making accurate, proper, decisions and/or judgement because of "matters". Matters can be described as a gravity pull on our lustful, desirable sensation that override our logical rational thinking skills. And because of that, it would believe that our judgement, decision-making are practically derived from other then our mind but from a "matters" perspective. Matter (material) is a dictation tool to one's who yearn or crave for "matter" (material) consumption in one form or another.

Next step will be to admit that you are powerless over matters. You must understand to acknowledge the effect that matters have upon you along with admitting that you are powerless over matters not just about yourself, but about the therapeutic process. Believe it or not you are already in a therapeutic process by acknowledging and admitting. That alone is the most psychological breakthrough that is required to proceed in this self-help book. As it is said, "knowing is half the battle". You are self-preservation and self-resolution without you even knowing it. Sometimes it takes us to have an assessment format that can be used for times when we are challenged whether it is mental or physical.

Second Exercise

Something else that will need to be welcome in this process is "understanding" the matter having control over our lives. We must be able to identify, dissect if needed as well as know how it plays out in our lives. This will give your therapeutic process more intense meaning.

Third Exercise

Acceptance is the goal in lines of a mature process. Any given episode in our lives that suggests challenges, is made for us to face the result whether we like it or not. Regardless of the outcome we must be willing to accept the result to take the giving lesson to its totality. Once all these measures are used and we accept responsibility, then we will be able to process any situation with a mature perspective. Owning your problems are one of the biggest things we will have to embrace, that is when we can move forward to fixing something that we now see and understand and "willing" to work on.

Fourth Exercise

Sacrifice will have to be made for this transition to become successful. The ironic thing that must be sacrificed is yes you guess it, material (matter) things in which the primary problem that causes distraction in our rational clear thinking. Not being able to think clearly is just one of the concerns, consequently it becomes a bigger problem when you start getting bad outcomes from our irrational thinking. We must begin by making a list of everything that plays a significant role in your life.

 Like for example, when we wake up to a new day, there are something or someone that comes to mind before our day get started. Sacrifice, secondly put next to the names of things and people on why they have tremendous effect on your life. To answer this question, you will have to answer a question inside a question. For example, I listed my favorite watch, while my watch has a strong effect on my thoughts because I misplaced my favorite watch and I wear it every day. Another example, I listed my girlfriend, next to that I put the reason why she has a strong effect on my thoughts is because we had an argument that causes us to not talk and I'm used to talking to her all day.

The source of energy and the lifeline are the matters of our thoughts and matters that can be distorted in our lives. Matters can also weaken and exhaust us from having a strong train of thought. It is practically impossible to have nothing on your mind when it is proven fact that our minds stay awake or in motion while we sleep in one form of a dream or reality, which later that becomes "matters" suppression.

Do you recall studying for a test or perhaps taking a test? If you clearly can, you remember how focus you were and why you were so focused. The occasion importance of the test played a big part that required dedication. Dedication is described as to devote to something, set aside for a divine purpose.

Now as we notice our minds set aside other "matters" for a define purpose which was the test. What would have to happen is we use the same formula as we did or do when we take tests.

Like I mentioned earlier, we only have one source of energy and that energy usually is divided into more than one thought, action, and verbal. Have you ever heard the paraphrase "one's who talk more do less and "ones" who do less talk more". Well, if you put some thought into it, you will find it to have some truth. The point I am trying to make is that this hypothetical scenario is an example of how energy is used.

Now to go back to the formula to use as when we take test, "prioritize thoughts" is what I will to call it, and suppression thoughts is also use as well. How it works is you practice with lists you made pertaining to what affects you and why. Then make a list of things and people that are important and/or priority to you and why it is important and/or priority. Usually when we have thoughts that are important and/or we tend to be clear and rational because those subjects require more attention and dedication. For example, I woke up getting ready for work and my girlfriend kept calling me, I was curious about what she wanted, however I suppressed those thoughts with my importance and/or priority thoughts.

I would like for you to use something of what effects your list to demonstrate. Second, use something or someone on your important and/or a priority list to use in your first demonstration; Now think about that one thing that affects you. Now suppress that thought by thinking about something important and/or a priority. Before you realize it, you are executing the "Mind over Matter". Practice makes perfect.

More Exercises

Step 1

Write out your favorite things and people you like
or love the most:

Step 2

Write out your favorite things and people and
why you love them the most:

Step 3

Write out what makes you most happy, and what
brings you joy:

Step 4

What makes you sad and mad?

Step 5

Write out person/people you are more comfortable with. Most likely the person/people you are more comfortable with will likely be the one you are more comfortable talking to.

Have a discussion with the aforesaid people and tell them you love them. Most likely, they will respond with "I love you too" This four-letter word is so huge it will immediately serve as an emotional therapeutic ignitor that will feed your self-esteem.

Step 6

Write down everything you like doing.

Step 7

Set your alarm on your phone on a morning daily basis to say something inspiring, wonderful, motivational, uplifting, to yourself. Also set your phone wallpaper to something or someone that's impressionable to your mind.

Step 8

Everyone has a theme song; Start your day off
with your uplifting theme song to start your day.

Step 9

Text or talk to someone you normally have absolutely no problem with before the night ends. The key to such transfer positive energy is to relate to someone that has a grip of stability in their life.

Step 10

If you are a believer and resonate with your Spirituality download and app of your favorite speaker and listen to him and her to get your day started and end your day with it as well.

Put on your wallpaper a favorite quote that motivates you.

Step 11

Open a door for someone and compliment someone. Give someone spare change. Text someone something positive every day. To receive positive feedback, do and show someone a good deed every day.

Step 12

Do something useful every day, example, Take
out trash for yourself or others.

Step 13

Remember the contributions you made for today.

Lastly

(Repeat all steps) and incorporate exercising daily. Essentially keep your body moving rather you at a gym or in your residence do commit to doing some form of exercise daily in your life.

Remember it's:

Mind

Over

Matter

Your Mind matters

&

You are in Control